MW00781650

All-Time Sports Records

FOOTBALL RECORDS

MARK WEAKLAND

BLACK
RABBIT
BOOKS

Bolt is published by Black Rabbit Books
P.O. Box 3263, Mankato, Minnesota, 56002.
www.blackrabbitbooks.com
Copyright © 2021 Black Rabbit Books

Jen Besel, editor; Catherine Cates, designer;
Omay Ayres, photo researcher

All rights reserved. No part of this book may be reproduced,
stored in a retrieval system or transmitted in any form or by any means,
electronic, mechanical, photocopying, recording, or otherwise, without written
permission from the publisher.

Library of Congress Cataloging-in-Publication Data
Names: Weakland, Mark, author.
Title: Football records / by Mark Weakland.
Other titles: Bolt (North Mankato, Minn.)
Description: Mankato, Minnesota : Bolt | Black Rabbit Books, 2021. |
Series: Bolt. All-time sports records | Includes webography. | Audience:
Ages: 4-12 years. | Audience: Grades: 4-6.
Identifiers: LCCN 2019028408 (print) | ISBN 9781623102418 (Hardcover) |
ISBN 9781644663370 (Paperback) | ISBN 9781623103354 (eBook)
Subjects: LCSH: Football—Records—United States—Juvenile literature. |
Football—United States—History—Juvenile literature. | Football
players—Rating of—Juvenile literature. | National Football
League—History—Juvenile literature.
Classification: LCC GV955 .W43 2021 (print) | LCC GV955 (ebook) |
DDC 796.33202/02—dc23
LC record available at https://lccn.loc.gov/2019028408
LC ebook record available at https://lccn.loc.gov/2019028409

Printed in the United States. 2/20

All records and statistics are current as of 2019.

Image Credits

Alamy: Cal Sport Media, 24; Jose
Luis Villegas, 6; McClatchy-Tribune, 12;
Tribune Content Agency LLC, 15; AP Images:
Al Messerschmidt Archive, 11; ASSOCIATED
PRESS, 12; CEK, 11; David J. Phillip, 28–29; Peter
Read Miller, Cover; Ryan Kang, 16–17; Scott Boehm,
14; Dreamstime: Jerry Coli, 1, 3, 11; Getty: George Silk,
10; Leo Mason/Popperfoto, 8–9; Newscom: MIKE SEGAR,
4–5; Shutterstock: Christos Georghiou, 26; ii-graphics,
16; kapona, 31; Oleksii Sidorov, 18–19; PSboom, 18–19;
Studio_G, 27; Todd Taulman Photography, 32; TotemArt,
26–27; winui, 10–11; tumblr.com: jonathandouglassims,
10; Twitter/spextcomponents.nfl.net: Kansas City Cheifs,
20; twitter.com: Green Bay Packers, 10;
Los Angeles Rams, 23
Every effort has been made to contact copyright
holders for material reproduced in this book.
Any omissions will be rectified in
subsequent printings if notice is
given to the publisher.

CONTENTS

CHAPTER 1

A Thrilling

GAME

The team lines up just a few yards from the goal line. The center hikes the ball. The **offense** rushes forward. The running back dashes ahead, legs pumping.

Football is a thrilling game. Great players make and break big records. Some records are so amazing, they might never be broken.

Most Career Receiving Yards

Jerry Rice	Larry Fitzgerald	Terrell Owens	Randy Moss	Isaac Bruce
22,895	16,279	15,934	15,292	15,208

CHAPTER 2

Unbelievable RECORDS

RECORD!

Most Career Receiving Yards 22,895

Some people think Jerry Rice was the greatest wide receiver ever. He was fast. He was strong and tall. His huge hands helped him catch passes while running and leaping. In his **career**, Rice gained 22,895 yards. No one else is even close.

Eric Dickerson was one of the NFL's greatest running backs. He was hard to catch as he dashed down the field. He set many records in his career. Some have been broken by others. But his record for rushing yards in a season still stands. In 1984, Dickerson ran for 2,105 yards.

RECORD!

Most Career Wins by a Coach **328**

Great coaches make great teams. These coaches have won the most in NFL history.

250

226

213

25
YEARS COACHING

Paul Brown

33
YEARS COACHING

Curly Lambeau

29
YEARS COACHING

Tom Landry

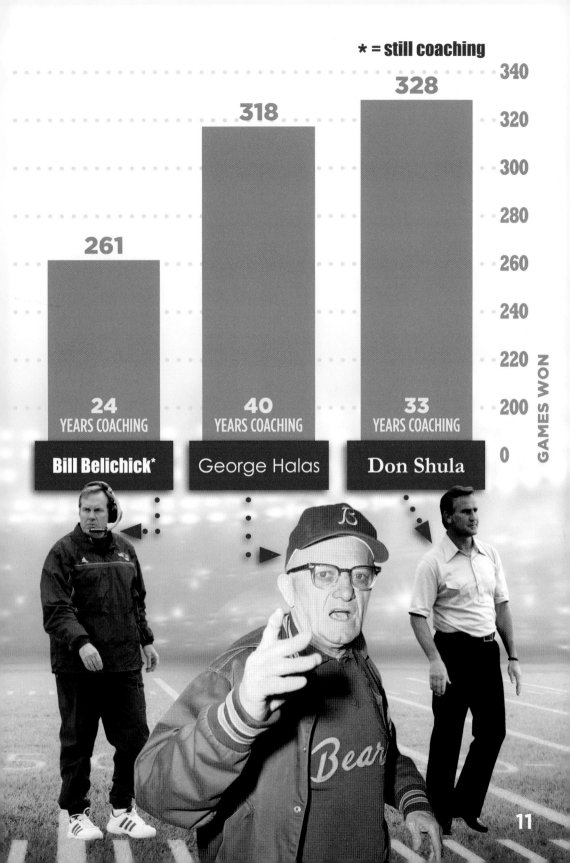

* = still coaching

340

328

320

318

300

280

261

260

240

220

24
YEARS COACHING

40
YEARS COACHING

33
YEARS COACHING

200

0

GAMES WON

Bill Belichick*

George Halas

Don Shula

Not-So-Good Records

Jim Marshall ran the ball 66 yards in the wrong direction. He scored for the other team!

The Tampa Bay Buccaneers lost a record 26 games in a row.

Brett Favre holds the record for most career **fumbles** with 166.

Sometimes great players have bad years. For George Blanda, 1962 was rotten. He threw 42 **interceptions** that year. Unfortunately, that's still a record.

Blanda did have many good years. And he set a lot of passing records. He was also a great kicker. He kicked more extra points than any other player in the NFL.

Game after game,
Brett Favre made
great plays. He
threw short
screens and long
bombs. He ran and
dived for touchdowns.
Favre holds many NFL
records. One record is
for most **consecutive**
games played. He played
297 games in a row.
He even played the day
after his father died.

RECORD!

Most Passes Thrown without an Interception 402

Aaron Rodgers is a pinpoint passer. • • •
In 2018, he threw 402 passes in a row
without one interception.

Tom Brady is known as a Super Bowl **legend**. He has six Super Bowl rings. He's also played more Super Bowls than any other player.

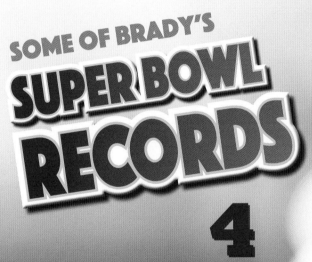

SOME OF BRADY'S

SUPER BOWL RECORDS

4
MOST SUPER BOWL MVP AWARDS

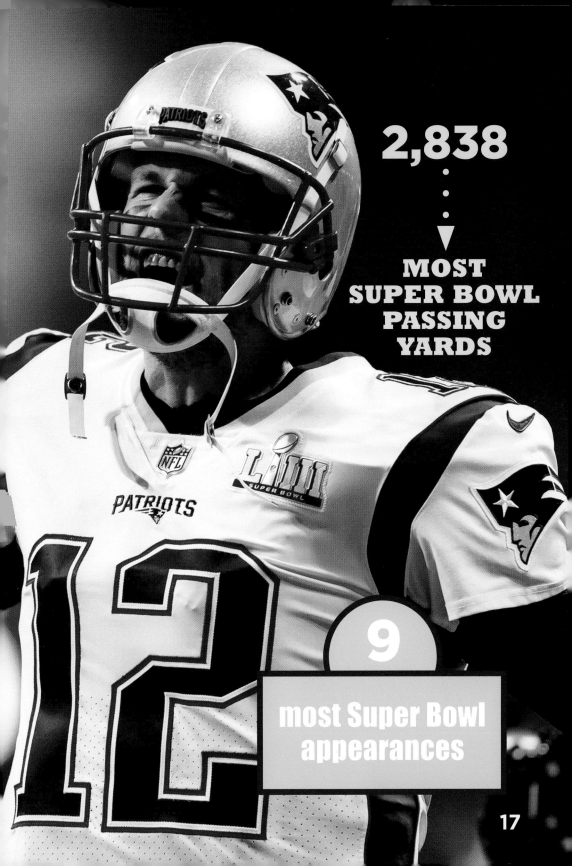

2,838
⋮
▼
MOST SUPER BOWL PASSING YARDS

9
most Super Bowl appearances

RECORD!
Most Team Super Bowl Wins **6**

The Pittsburgh Steelers held the record for most Super Bowl wins for years. But the New England Patriots tied it in 2019.

GREEN BAY PACKERS
4 SUPER BOWL WINS

SAN FRANCISCO 49ERS
5 SUPER BOWL WINS

PITTSBURGH STEELERS
6 SUPER BOWL WINS

NEW YORK GIANTS
4 SUPER BOWL WINS

DALLAS COWBOYS
5 SUPER BOWL WINS

NEW ENGLAND PATRIOTS
6 SUPER BOWL WINS

Some people say Nor Willey made 17 **sacks** in one 1952 game. But sacks were not tracked until 1982. And no one can find video of the game to prove the record.

RECORD!
Most Sacks in One Game 7

· · · · · ·Derrick Thomas had one game that
was like no other. Time and time again,
he rushed the quarterback. Time and
time again, he pulled him down before
he could pass the ball. By the end of
the game, Thomas had seven sacks.
That's a tough record to beat.

The year was 1951. It was the first game of the season. Norm Van Brocklin threw the ball over and over again. His receivers caught more than half his passes. By the end of the game, Van Brocklin had thrown for 554 yards. It was the greatest passing day in NFL history. More than 60 years later, the record still stands.

23

Many fans say Adam Vinatieri is the best NFL field goal kicker ever. He kicked goals in four Super Bowls. In two of those, his kick won the game. In his career, he kicked 582 field goals. That's a record.

Vinatieri has scored more than 2,600 points in his career. That's also a record. No other player is close.

RECORD!

Longest Field Goal Ever Made **64 YARDS**

The record for longest field goal used to be 63 yards. It was set four times by four different players. Then Matt Prater kicked a field goal one yard longer.

64 YARDS
MATT PRATER
Denver Broncos
2013

63 YARDS
DAVID AKERS
San Francisco 49ers
2012

63 YARDS
TOM DEMPSEY
New Orleans Saints
1970

63 YARDS
JASON ELAM
Denver Broncos
1998

63 YARDS
SEBASTIAN JANIKOWSKI
Oakland Raiders
2011

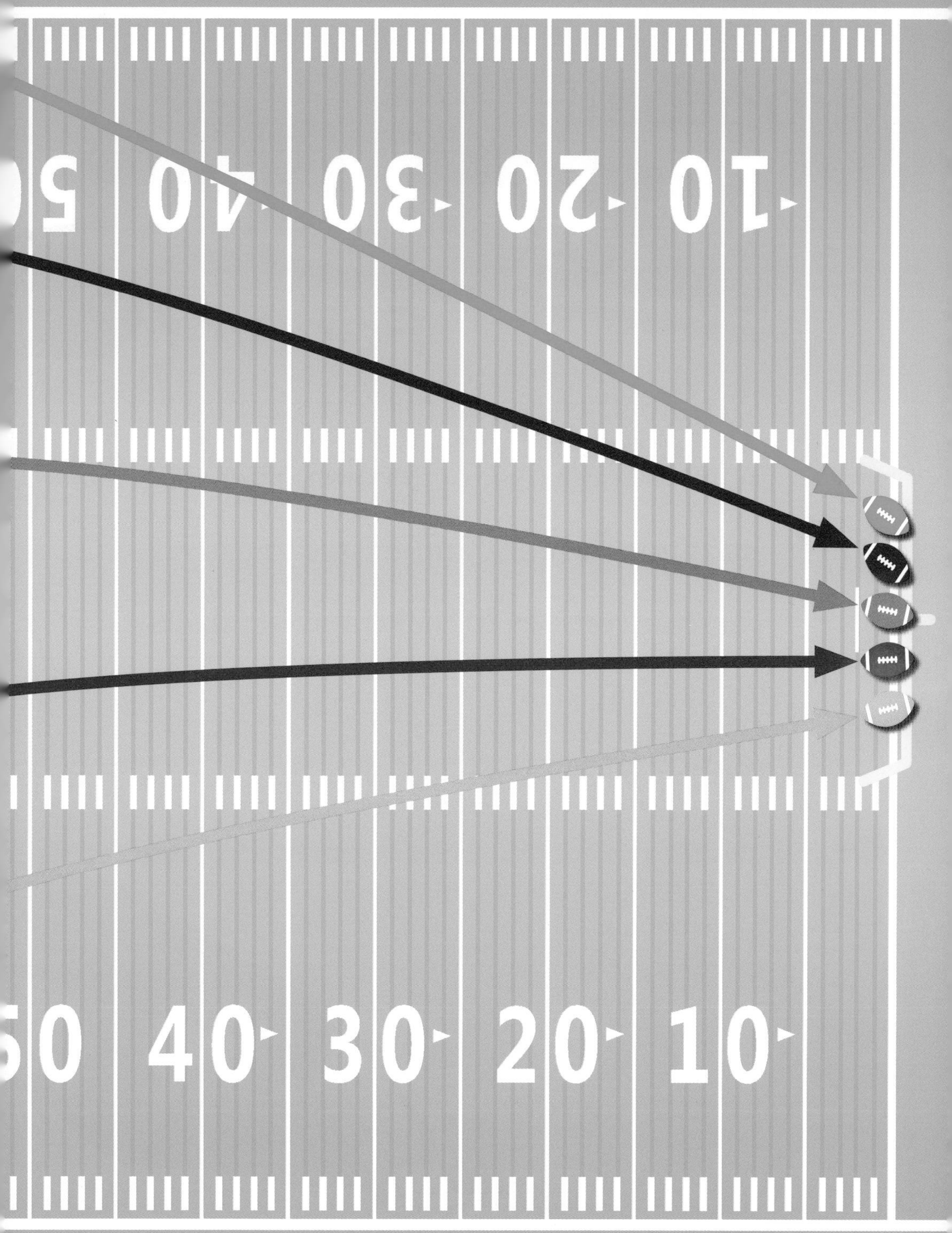

40
30
20
10

CHAPTER 3

Football RECORDS Forever

Football is a sport that's perfect for making and breaking records. There are punts to block and passes to throw. There are tackles to make and handoffs to fake. Fans can't wait to see what records are set next.

GLOSSARY

career (kuh-REER)—a period of time spent in a job

consecutive (kuhn-SEK-yoo-tiv)—following one after the other in order

fumble (FUM-buhl)—to fail to catch or hold the ball

interception (in-tur-SEP-shun)—a catch made by a player from the opposing team

legend (LEJ-uhnd)—a famous or important person who is known for doing something extremely well

offense (AW-fens)—the group of players in control of the ball trying to score points

sack (SAK)—a tackle of the quarterback before he or she crosses the line of scrimmage

screen (SKREEN)—a short pass to a receiver who is protected by blockers

BOOKS

Bowker, Paul. *Best Super Bowl Records.* Best of the Super Bowl. Mankato, MN: 12-Story Library, 2019.

Clausen-Grace, Nicki, and Jeff Grace. *Football Teams by the Numbers.* Got Game. Mankato: MN: Black Rabbit Books, 2018.

Morey, Allan. *Football Records.* Incredible Sports Records. Minneapolis: Bellwether Media, Inc., 2018.

WEBSITES

Facts about Football for Kids
www.dkfindout.com/us/sports/football/

Football
www.ducksters.com/sports/football.php

Football
www.sikids.com/football

INDEX